Mastering DeepSeek-v3

Unlocking Advanced Features for Expert Users

CONTENTS

Chapter 3: Exploring Advanced Search Algorithms

- **Machine Learning-Enhanced Search**: How DeepSeek-v3 uses ML to enhance search accuracy.
- **Custom Search Filters**: Setting up and utilizing custom filters for tailored results.
- **SEO Keywords**: DeepSeek search algorithms, machine learning search, custom search filters, advanced search techniques.

Chapter 4: Optimizing Results with DeepSeek-v3's Advanced Features

- **Search Relevance Tuning**: How to fine-tune the relevance of search results using advanced settings.
- **Custom Data Integration**: Integrating third-party data sources for more accurate results.
- **SEO Keywords**: DeepSeek advanced optimization, search relevance, data integration, custom data sources.

Chapter 5: Automating Tasks with DeepSeek-v3

- **Automation Setup**: Setting up DeepSeek-v3 to automate searches and tasks.

- **Batch Processing**: How to perform large-scale automated queries using batch processing tools.
- **SEO Keywords**: DeepSeek automation, batch processing with DeepSeek, automating tasks with DeepSeek-v3.

Chapter 6: Using DeepSeek-v3's API for Advanced Features

- **API Introduction**: An overview of DeepSeek-v3's API capabilities and potential uses.
- **Creating Custom Scripts**: Writing scripts that leverage DeepSeek's API for specialized use cases.
- **SEO Keywords**: DeepSeek API, using DeepSeek API, advanced DeepSeek scripting.

Chapter 7: Monitoring and Analytics Tools in DeepSeek-v3

- **Analytics Dashboard**: Understanding the advanced analytics dashboard to track usage and performance.
- **Real-time Monitoring**: Using the real-time monitoring feature for immediate feedback on tasks.

- **SEO Keywords**: DeepSeek analytics, real-time monitoring, DeepSeek performance tracking, analytics dashboard.

Chapter 8: Troubleshooting and Optimization Tips

- **Performance Issues**: Common problems and how to resolve them.
- **Improving Search Accuracy**: Fine-tuning DeepSeek-v3 for even better results.
- **SEO Keywords**: DeepSeek troubleshooting, optimizing DeepSeek, DeepSeek performance tips.

Chapter 9: Best Practices for Mastering DeepSeek-v3

- **Expert Tips**: Tricks and insights from advanced users on getting the most from DeepSeek-v3.
- **Case Studies**: Real-world examples of successful DeepSeek implementations.
- **SEO Keywords**: DeepSeek expert tips, mastering DeepSeek-v3, DeepSeek case studies, advanced user strategies.

Chapter 10: The Future of DeepSeek and What's Next

- **Upcoming Features**: A sneak peek at future updates and features of DeepSeek.

- **Preparing for Changes**: How to stay ahead of the curve and integrate future improvements.
- **SEO Keywords**: future of DeepSeek, upcoming DeepSeek features, DeepSeek v4, staying ahead with DeepSeek.

Chapter 11: Scaling DeepSeek-V3 for Large-Scale Applications

1. **Introduction to Scaling DeepSeek-V3**
2. **Cloud-based Deployment**
3. **Distributed Computing with DeepSeek-V3**
4. **Performance Tuning and Optimization**

Chapter 12: Security and Privacy in DeepSeek-V3

- **Introduction to Security and Privacy**
- **DeepSeek-V3 Security Features**
- **Vulnerabilities and Risk Management**
- **Best Practices for Secure Use of DeepSeek-V3**

Mastering DeepSeek-v3

Unlocking Advanced Features for Expert Users

Chapter 1: Introduction to DeepSeek-v3

Overview of DeepSeek-v3

DeepSeek-v3 is the latest iteration of the DeepSeek search engine, a robust tool designed to cater to the needs of professionals and experts across a wide range of industries. As a powerful data search engine, DeepSeek-v3 is engineered for precision, speed, and efficiency, making it an invaluable asset for individuals and businesses looking to extract actionable insights from vast pools of data.

What sets **DeepSeek-v3** apart from its predecessors is its enhanced search algorithms, which leverage cutting-edge artificial intelligence (AI) and machine learning (ML) models. These advancements allow users to query vast datasets with unprecedented accuracy, making it easier to uncover relevant information even in the most complex data environments.

DeepSeek-v3's capabilities go beyond traditional search engines. It integrates seamlessly with various data sources, including both structured and unstructured data, allowing users to perform intricate searches across databases, file systems, and even real-time streaming data.

Key Features of DeepSeek-v3:

- **Enhanced Search Algorithms**: DeepSeek-v3's advanced AI and ML algorithms ensure that results are not just relevant but also optimized for the user's specific needs.
- **Customizable Filters and Data Integrations**: Users can tailor searches using custom filters and integrate with third-party data sources for more refined results.
- **Real-Time Search Results**: DeepSeek-v3 provides instant, actionable search results for real-time data streams.
- **Automation and Batch Processing**: The tool offers powerful automation capabilities, enabling users to schedule tasks and process large datasets in batches.
- **Comprehensive API**: DeepSeek-v3's API allows developers to create customized search applications, integrating seamlessly into existing workflows and systems.

Applications Across Industries

DeepSeek-v3 is versatile, serving multiple industries where data analysis and search optimization are critical. Here are just a few of its use cases:

- **Healthcare**: Medical professionals use DeepSeek-v3 to search vast medical databases for research purposes or to find patient records more effectively.
- **Finance**: Analysts rely on DeepSeek-v3 to perform data-driven analysis across financial reports, market trends, and historical data.
- **E-commerce**: Retailers use DeepSeek-v3 to enhance product search capabilities, improving customer experience by providing faster and more accurate results.
- **Legal**: Legal professionals use DeepSeek-v3 for searching case files, statutes, and legal databases with custom filters for case-specific queries.

With the ability to scale across different sectors, DeepSeek-v3 is revolutionizing the way data-driven industries approach search and analysis.

Why Choose DeepSeek-v3?

DeepSeek-v3 offers numerous advantages over its previous versions and other alternatives available in the market. Let's dive into why **DeepSeek-v3** should be your go-to tool for advanced data search needs:

1. Superior Accuracy and Precision

DeepSeek-v3's enhanced AI-powered search capabilities ensure that results are not only accurate but also highly relevant. The tool is designed to minimize false positives and filter out irrelevant data, allowing users to zero in on what really matters.

2. Faster Search Results

Gone are the days of waiting for long search queries to process. DeepSeek-v3 utilizes optimized algorithms that significantly reduce search time, making it the ideal solution for professionals who need fast, actionable insights.

3. Greater Flexibility and Customization

DeepSeek-v3 provides users with customizable filters, allowing for more granular control over search parameters. This flexibility empowers users to tailor searches based on industry-specific criteria, ensuring more personalized and relevant results.

4. Integration with Third-Party Data

Unlike many search engines, DeepSeek-v3 offers robust integration capabilities with external data sources. Whether you're pulling data from APIs, cloud storage, or other databases, DeepSeek-v3 ensures smooth, real-time data connectivity.

5. Powerful Automation Features

For users working with large datasets, DeepSeek-v3 simplifies the process of batch processing and automating routine tasks. This feature is especially useful for data analysts, researchers, and professionals working with continuous data streams.

6. Enhanced User Experience

With a user-friendly interface, DeepSeek-v3 offers an intuitive and seamless experience for both novice and expert users. Its clean design and easy navigation reduce the learning curve, allowing users to dive straight into using its advanced features.

Benefits of DeepSeek-v3 Over Previous Versions and Alternatives

While earlier versions of DeepSeek laid the foundation for a strong data search engine, **DeepSeek-v3** builds on this legacy with notable improvements. Here's why DeepSeek-v3 stands out:

- **Advanced AI and ML Models**: These new algorithms improve accuracy and efficiency, setting DeepSeek-v3 apart from older versions that relied on less sophisticated search techniques.
- **Enhanced Scalability**: DeepSeek-v3 can handle larger datasets more effectively, supporting enterprise-level data searches, something earlier versions struggled with.
- **Improved Integration Capabilities**: With third-party integration now a key feature, DeepSeek-v3 surpasses its predecessors by connecting seamlessly to more diverse data sources, offering more comprehensive search results.
- **Automation Features**: Where previous versions required manual intervention for large-scale data processing, DeepSeek-v3 automates many processes, saving users time and effort.

Chapter 2: Setting Up DeepSeek-v3 for Advanced Use

Installation Process

Getting started with **DeepSeek-v3** begins with the installation process. Whether you're installing on a local machine or deploying on a server, the following guide will walk you through the steps for a successful installation.

System Requirements

Before you begin, make sure your system meets the necessary requirements to ensure optimal performance. Here's a breakdown of the minimum and recommended system requirements for **DeepSeek-v3**:

Minimum System Requirements:

- **Operating System**: Windows 10 or later, macOS 10.12 or later, or a Linux-based system (Ubuntu 18.04 or later).
- **Processor**: Intel Core i5 or equivalent (or better).
- **RAM**: 8GB of RAM.
- **Storage**: 20GB of free disk space (SSD preferred for faster performance).
- **Network**: Broadband internet connection for cloud-based operations and updates.
- **Software Dependencies**:

- o Python 3.7 or later.
- o Java 8 or later (for certain backend operations).
- o Docker (optional, but recommended for cloud-based deployment).

Recommended System Requirements:

- **Operating System**: Windows 11, macOS 11 (Big Sur), or a 64-bit Linux distribution (Ubuntu 20.04 or later).
- **Processor**: Intel Core i7 or equivalent, or higher for faster processing.
- **RAM**: 16GB of RAM or more.
- **Storage**: 50GB of free SSD space for faster data processing.
- **Network**: Gigabit Ethernet for optimal data transfer.
- **Software Dependencies**: Same as minimum system requirements with additional cloud management tools for enterprise use.

Step-by-Step Installation Guide

1. **Download the DeepSeek-v3 Installer**
   - o Visit the official DeepSeek website or the designated repository.
   - o Choose the version of DeepSeek-v3 suitable for your operating system (Windows, macOS, or Linux).

- o Download the installer package (.exe for Windows, .dmg for macOS, or .tar.gz for Linux).

2. **Run the Installer**
   - o On Windows, double-click the .exe file to launch the installation wizard.
   - o On macOS, open the .dmg file and drag the DeepSeek-v3 application to the Applications folder.
   - o On Linux, extract the .tar.gz package and follow the installation instructions in the README file.

3. **Accept License Agreement**
   - o Review the license agreement and accept it to continue the installation.

4. **Select Installation Directory**
   - o Choose the directory where you want DeepSeek-v3 to be installed. The default directory is usually sufficient, but you can select a custom directory if preferred.

5. **Install Dependencies**
   - o The installer will automatically check for necessary dependencies and install them if they are missing. This may include Python, Java, or Docker.

6. **Complete Installation**
   - o After the installer finishes setting up DeepSeek-v3, click "Finish" to complete the installation process.

You may need to restart your machine to apply changes.

7. **Verify Installation**
   ○ To verify that the installation was successful, open a terminal or command prompt and type:

   css
   CopierModifier
   deepseek-v3 --version

   ○ This command should display the current version of DeepSeek-v3, confirming that the installation was successful.

Initial Configuration

Once **DeepSeek-v3** is installed, it's time to configure it for optimal performance. Proper configuration ensures that DeepSeek-v3 runs efficiently and meets your specific needs. Here's how to get started:

Step 1: Launch the DeepSeek-v3 Application

- On Windows, you can launch DeepSeek-v3 by finding it in the Start Menu.
- On macOS, navigate to the Applications folder and click the DeepSeek-v3 icon.
- On Linux, open a terminal and type:

CopierModifier
deepseek-v3

Step 2: Configure General Settings

When you launch DeepSeek-v3 for the first time, the system will prompt you to configure general settings. Here's a step-by-step guide:

1. **User Profile Setup**:
   - Enter your user information, such as name and email, to personalize your DeepSeek-v3 experience.
   - This information is stored locally for your reference and access to premium features.
2. **System Preferences**:
   - Set your preferred language and time zone.
   - Choose the default data storage location (local or cloud-based storage).
3. **Networking Settings**:
   - Configure proxy settings if you're working behind a firewall or in a restricted network environment.
   - DeepSeek-v3 automatically detects and configures proxy settings, but manual configuration is available if needed.
4. **Advanced Features**:

o Enable or disable advanced features like machine learning models, real-time search, and API access, depending on your usage needs.

o For optimal performance, enable caching and allow DeepSeek-v3 to use more system resources if necessary.

Step 3: Configure Data Sources

DeepSeek-v3 supports a wide range of data sources, and configuring them is essential for personalized and efficient searches. Here's how to set it up:

1. **Add External Data Sources**:
   o You can link external databases, APIs, cloud storage services (e.g., AWS S3, Google Cloud), or file systems.
   o To add a data source, click the "Add Source" button in the settings menu, select the appropriate type (e.g., SQL database, CSV file), and provide connection details.
2. **Customize Search Filters**:
   o Customize your search filters to streamline data retrieval. Set up filters based on content type,

keywords, or data properties such as size or date of modification.

3. **Set Up Automated Tasks**:

   o Schedule automated searches, data indexing, or batch processing tasks. DeepSeek-v3 allows you to define regular intervals for executing tasks, saving you time in managing large datasets.

Step 4: Test Configuration

Once you've completed the setup, run a test search to ensure everything is functioning as expected. You can use the **Quick Search** feature to test different configurations, ensuring the results match your expectations.

- **Run a Basic Search**: Enter a common query to verify that DeepSeek-v3 is pulling results from your selected data sources.
- **Test Real-Time Search**: If enabled, test real-time search features to ensure the data stream is processed efficiently.

This chapter provides a comprehensive guide to setting up **DeepSeek-v3** for advanced use, from installation to configuration. Following these steps ensures that you are prepared to leverage DeepSeek-v3's powerful features and customize the tool to fit your specific needs.

Chapter 3: Exploring Advanced Search Algorithms

Machine Learning-Enhanced Search

One of the standout features of **DeepSeek-v3** is its integration of machine learning (ML) algorithms to improve search accuracy and efficiency. Traditional search engines rely on pre-defined parameters, but DeepSeek-v3's ML-enhanced search capabilities are designed to learn from user behavior and adapt to deliver more relevant results over time.

How DeepSeek-v3 Uses Machine Learning for Search

DeepSeek-v3 uses machine learning models to enhance the search process in several ways:

1. **Contextual Understanding**:
   - By leveraging natural language processing (NLP) techniques, DeepSeek-v3 interprets the meaning behind your search queries. Instead of relying solely on keywords, it understands the context of a query and returns results that are contextually relevant.
   - For example, a query like "how to improve search results" will be interpreted not just as a request for

specific keywords, but as a broader need for strategies to enhance search efficiency, bringing up advanced search techniques, guides, and optimization tips.

2. **Predictive Search Results**:
   - Machine learning models predict what users are most likely to search for based on past behavior, query patterns, and preferences. This allows DeepSeek-v3 to provide **predictive search suggestions** in real-time, making the search process quicker and more accurate.

3. **Personalized Search**:
   - DeepSeek-v3's ML algorithms personalize results based on your search history, preferences, and interactions with the platform. As you use the system more, the search engine refines its understanding of your needs and adjusts the ranking of results to better align with your interests and priorities.

4. **Auto-Correction and Synonym Recognition**:
   - DeepSeek-v3's ML engine recognizes spelling errors and suggests corrections on the fly. Additionally, it understands synonyms and variations in phrasing, ensuring that

even if you don't phrase your search query perfectly, the system will still return relevant results.

Training the Machine Learning Model

The more you interact with **DeepSeek-v3**, the smarter its search algorithm becomes. The system collects feedback from your searches, continually refining the machine learning model to provide even more accurate results. If you regularly use specific filters or data sources, DeepSeek-v3 will prioritize these elements in future searches.

Custom Search Filters

Another powerful feature of **DeepSeek-v3** is the ability to create and utilize **custom search filters**, allowing you to fine-tune your results to meet specific criteria.

Creating Custom Search Filters

1. **Filter by Data Type**:
   - You can create filters based on the type of data you're looking for. For example, you can filter by file format (e.g., PDFs, images, text files) or by document type (e.g., reports, presentations, spreadsheets).

2. **Time-Based Filters**:
    o DeepSeek-v3 allows you to specify date ranges for your searches, helping you focus on the most recent data or historical records. This is especially useful when working with time-sensitive or project-specific data.
    o You can set filters like "Created after" or "Modified before" to narrow your search to a specific window.
3. **Advanced Boolean Filters**:
    o For expert users, **DeepSeek-v3** supports advanced Boolean operators to combine multiple filters. Use operators like AND, OR, NOT, and parentheses to create complex queries that extract the most relevant results.
    o For example, you might search for "machine learning AND deep learning NOT tensorflow" to exclude certain results from your search.
4. **Data Source-Specific Filters**:
    o You can set up filters that are specific to particular data sources (e.g., filtering by database type, cloud storage, or server). This allows you to tailor searches for specific platforms or systems.

5. **Tagging and Labeling**:
    - o For larger datasets, you can use tags and labels to organize data, making it easier to search through them. This is particularly useful when dealing with vast amounts of data stored across various platforms.

Applying Filters in DeepSeek-v3

Once your filters are set up, you can apply them in the search query interface. You can choose whether to apply a single filter or combine multiple filters for more granular results. The filters can be saved as templates, which makes it easier to run similar searches in the future without having to reconfigure them each time.

For instance, if you frequently search for customer service reports from a particular database and within a certain date range, you can save that as a template and reuse it as needed.

Example of Custom Filter Use:

If you want to retrieve recent marketing reports in PDF format from the last quarter but exclude certain databases, you would set the following filters:

- **File Type**: PDF
- **Date Modified**: Last 3 months
- **Exclude Data Source**: MarketingDB_v1

By applying these filters, DeepSeek-v3 will only return the relevant results, saving you time and effort in manually sifting through irrelevant data.

Advanced Search Techniques

DeepSeek-v3 provides users with various advanced search techniques to maximize the platform's capabilities. Here are a few methods you can use to refine your searches further:

1. **Wildcard Search**:
   - If you're unsure of the exact phrasing or spelling of a search term, you can use wildcards (* or ?) to broaden your search. For example:
     - Searching for "machine * learning" will return results that include both "machine learning" and "machine vision learning."
     - Searching for "reco?gnition" will return results for both "recognition" and "recognising."
2. **Fuzzy Search**:
   - **DeepSeek-v3** supports fuzzy searching, where minor typos or

misspellings are ignored, and relevant results are returned. This feature is powered by ML algorithms that understand the intent behind the query, even when there are errors in spelling or word choice.

3. **Natural Language Queries**:
   - Instead of using rigid keyword-based searches, you can perform searches in natural language. For example, typing "show me reports on machine learning from last year" will return results that best match this query, even though it's not structured like a traditional keyword search.

4. **Proximity Search**:
   - DeepSeek-v3 allows you to search for terms that appear close to each other within a specified distance. For example, if you search for "artificial intelligence" within 5 words of "applications," you'll get results where those two terms are close together, making your search more precise.

Chapter 4: Optimizing Results with DeepSeek-v3's Advanced Features

Search Relevance Tuning

To ensure that your search results are as accurate and relevant as possible, **DeepSeek-v3** provides a range of advanced settings that allow you to fine-tune the relevance of your search outcomes. Understanding how to adjust these settings can significantly improve the efficiency of your searches, helping you to retrieve the most pertinent data for your needs.

Fine-Tuning Search Relevance

DeepSeek-v3's advanced search algorithms take several factors into account when determining the relevance of search results. As an expert user, you can further influence these factors by adjusting the following settings:

1. **Boosting and Demoting Keywords**:
   - **Keyword Boosting**: If certain keywords are more important than others, you can boost their relevance within the search results. By assigning a higher weight to specific terms, you can ensure that results containing those keywords appear higher in the ranking.

o **Keyword Demotion**: Conversely, if certain keywords are less important or irrelevant to your search, you can demote them. This will reduce their influence on the relevance scoring, ensuring that other factors are prioritized.

For example, if you're searching for "cloud computing," but want to prioritize results that focus on "security," you can boost the term "security" while demoting less relevant terms such as "networking."

2. **Adjusting Result Ranking Based on Relevance**:
   o DeepSeek-v3 allows you to configure how results are ranked. You can set preferences such as ranking based on freshness, authority, or the amount of content a result contains.
   o For instance, if you're looking for the most up-to-date research papers, you can adjust the settings to rank results based on their publication date rather than the general relevance of keywords.
3. **Contextual Relevance**:
   o DeepSeek-v3 goes beyond keyword matching by using contextual relevance. This setting helps the

system understand how search terms relate to each other in context, rather than just individual occurrences. For example, when searching for "climate change solutions," the system will prioritize results discussing actionable solutions rather than just mentions of the term.

4. **Synonym Recognition and Expansion**:
   - By enabling **synonym recognition**, you can help DeepSeek-v3 understand that certain terms are interchangeable. This ensures that synonyms like "AI" and "artificial intelligence" are treated as equal in relevance, leading to broader yet more accurate results.
   - You can customize the list of synonyms within the settings to ensure that the system understands the specific terminology you're working with.

Result Filtering and Relevance Thresholds

Another way to fine-tune search results is by applying **relevance thresholds**. This allows you to set a minimum relevance score for the results you receive. If a result falls below the set threshold, it will not appear in your search results, ensuring that only the most relevant data is returned.

For instance, you might set the relevance threshold to 80%, meaning that only results that score at least 80% relevance will be included, filtering out less pertinent data.

Custom Data Integration

One of the most powerful features of **DeepSeek-v3** is its ability to integrate third-party data sources into the search process. By incorporating external data sources, you can vastly improve the accuracy and comprehensiveness of your search results, especially when dealing with specialized or niche topics.

How to Integrate Custom Data Sources

DeepSeek-v3 allows you to connect to a variety of data sources, including internal databases, external APIs, and cloud storage platforms, to augment the search process.

1. **Adding APIs for Real-Time Data**:
   o You can integrate **real-time data sources** via API connections, which will enable DeepSeek-v3 to access up-to-date information across a wide

range of domains. For example, integrating a financial data API can help you search for real-time stock market trends and financial news.

2. **Connecting Databases**:
   - If you have proprietary data stored in external databases (SQL, NoSQL, etc.), DeepSeek-v3 allows you to **link those databases directly** to the search platform. This integration ensures that DeepSeek-v3 can query your internal systems and retrieve relevant data alongside web-based content.

3. **Cloud Storage Integration**:
   - DeepSeek-v3 can also sync with cloud storage services like Google Drive, Dropbox, and AWS S3, enabling you to search through documents, spreadsheets, and other files stored in these services. By integrating these cloud platforms, you can make your search results more comprehensive by including data stored in personal or enterprise cloud environments.

4. **Custom Data Sets**:
   - For niche or highly specific data, you can upload **custom datasets** directly into DeepSeek-v3. This allows you to conduct searches across highly

specialized collections of information, improving the precision of your queries.

o For example, if you have a dataset of medical records or scientific papers, you can upload it into DeepSeek-v3 and integrate it into the search process for specialized searches in those areas.

Benefits of Custom Data Integration

- **Enhanced Accuracy**: By integrating specific data sources, you can improve the accuracy of your search results, especially when dealing with technical or industry-specific information.
- **Time Efficiency**: Searching within a highly relevant, customized dataset or source can dramatically reduce the time spent sifting through unrelated or generic content.
- **Comprehensive Results**: With multiple data sources integrated, you can ensure that your search is as comprehensive as possible, providing you with insights from both external web sources and internal data repositories.

Example of Custom Data Integration

Imagine you're conducting research on machine learning techniques in healthcare. By integrating data from a **medical research database** and an **AI-related API**, you can retrieve highly specific and relevant results, such as research papers on ML applications in medicine, datasets for training AI models, and current news on AI-driven healthcare innovations.

Chapter 5: Automating Tasks with DeepSeek-v3

Automation Setup

One of the standout features of **DeepSeek-v3** is its ability to automate repetitive tasks, making your workflows more efficient and reducing manual input. Automation setup in DeepSeek-v3 allows you to configure searches and actions that can run independently, saving time and effort. In this section, we will walk through the key steps to set up and optimize your automation processes.

Step 1: Accessing Automation Settings

To get started, you will need to access the **automation settings** within DeepSeek-v3's interface. Typically found under the **Settings** or **Advanced Settings** section, this area contains all the necessary tools to configure automation.

1. **Login to your DeepSeek-v3 Account**: Ensure you are logged in to access all features.
2. **Navigate to Automation Settings**: Locate the automation tab from the dashboard or settings menu.
3. **Enable Automation**: Toggle the automation feature on to allow DeepSeek-v3 to run scheduled tasks automatically.

Step 2: Defining Tasks to Automate

Once automation is enabled, you can begin setting up tasks for automation. DeepSeek-v3 allows you to automate various actions, including:

- **Search Queries**: You can program DeepSeek-v3 to run searches at specified intervals or triggers, automatically retrieving the latest data based on your pre-set criteria.
- **Reporting**: Automate the generation of search reports, such as summaries of findings or data analytics, to be delivered at regular intervals (daily, weekly, etc.).
- **Data Retrieval**: Set up automated processes to pull specific types of data at certain times, reducing the need for constant manual searches.

Step 3: Setting Schedules

To ensure your tasks run consistently without requiring your intervention, DeepSeek-v3 enables **scheduling**. You can define when and how often certain tasks should execute:

- **Time-Based Scheduling**: Choose exact times, such as daily at 9:00 AM or weekly every Friday at noon.
- **Event-Based Triggers**: Set up automation triggers based on specific events. For

example, you can automate a search when new data is uploaded to your server or an external source.

Step 4: Reviewing Automation Logs

DeepSeek-v3 generates **automation logs** that allow you to monitor the performance of each automated task. You can track:

- The success or failure of automated searches
- Task execution times
- Errors or issues encountered during automated processes

Automation logs help in fine-tuning the tasks and ensuring everything is running smoothly.

Batch Processing: Performing Large-Scale Automated Queries

Batch processing is an essential feature when dealing with large volumes of data. **DeepSeek-v3** allows you to execute bulk queries or searches in batches, automating the entire process for high-efficiency, large-scale operations.

What is Batch Processing?

Batch processing involves executing multiple queries or actions in a single task. This is particularly useful when you need to retrieve data from various sources or perform several similar searches at once.

Setting Up Batch Processing in DeepSeek-v3

1. **Prepare Your Batch Queries**: Compile all the queries you want to run in a single file (CSV, Excel, etc.) or define them within DeepSeek-v3's batch processing interface. Each entry in the batch file should represent a unique query.
2. **Configure Batch Settings**:
    o **Execution Frequency**: You can choose whether the batch should run once, daily, or at custom intervals.
    o **Result Output**: Decide how you want the results to be outputted. Options might include storing them in a local file, exporting them to cloud storage, or sending reports via email.
3. **Start the Batch Process**: Once the batch configuration is complete, initiate the batch processing task. DeepSeek-v3 will automatically execute the queries in sequence or parallel, depending on your settings.

Benefits of Batch Processing with DeepSeek-v3

- **Efficiency**: Automates the repetitive task of running multiple searches individually, allowing you to focus on other important work.
- **Time-Saving**: Instead of running each search manually, DeepSeek-v3 processes multiple queries in the background, returning results quickly.
- **Consistency**: Automating batch queries ensures that all searches follow the same parameters, delivering consistent results across all executions.
- **Scalability**: Ideal for situations where you need to scale your operations quickly. Whether you're searching through hundreds or thousands of data points, DeepSeek-v3 handles it effortlessly.

Example of Batch Processing

Imagine you need to gather the latest market data from several websites across different sectors (e.g., finance, technology, healthcare). Instead of performing each search individually, you can set up a batch process where DeepSeek-v3 runs each query for you. The results are then compiled into a single report for easy review and analysis.

Chapter 6: Using DeepSeek-v3's API for Advanced Features

API Introduction: Unlocking the Power of DeepSeek-v3's API

One of the most powerful tools in **DeepSeek-v3** for expert users is its **Application Programming Interface (API)**. The API allows you to extend the functionality of DeepSeek-v3 beyond the traditional user interface, enabling you to integrate DeepSeek's advanced features directly into your applications, workflows, and automation systems.

What is an API?

An **API** is a set of protocols and tools that allows different software applications to communicate with each other. In the case of DeepSeek-v3, the API enables developers and users to interact with the platform programmatically, automating searches, integrating data, and customizing workflows without needing to manually access the interface.

DeepSeek-v3's API supports various operations, including:

- **Search Queries**: Programmatically run searches and retrieve results.

- **Data Integration**: Seamlessly connect third-party data sources to DeepSeek-v3 for enhanced results.
- **Automation**: Create custom automation workflows that integrate with other platforms.

The flexibility provided by the API makes it ideal for advanced users who require fine-grained control over their search operations or need to integrate DeepSeek-v3 with other software or systems.

Key Benefits of Using DeepSeek-v3's API

- **Customization**: Tailor your searches and workflows to suit your exact needs.
- **Integration**: Link DeepSeek-v3 with other systems, databases, or platforms to consolidate data and automate processes.
- **Efficiency**: Perform bulk queries and handle large datasets more efficiently than through the UI.
- **Scalability**: Scale your operations by automating tasks and integrating DeepSeek-v3 into enterprise-level systems.

Creating Custom Scripts: Leveraging DeepSeek-v3's API for Specialized Use Cases

With DeepSeek-v3's API, you can write custom scripts that automate searches, process data, and enhance the platform's capabilities for your specific use cases. Whether you're building a small script to retrieve data periodically or developing a large-scale automation system, the API makes it possible.

Step 1: Understanding the API Documentation

Before diving into scripting, familiarize yourself with the **API documentation**. DeepSeek-v3 provides comprehensive documentation that outlines:

- **Endpoints**: The various functions available, such as search, data retrieval, and report generation.
- **Authentication**: How to securely authenticate your API requests using API keys or OAuth tokens.
- **Parameters**: What inputs are required for each endpoint and the structure of responses.
- **Rate Limits**: The number of requests you can make within a certain time period to prevent overloading the system.

Step 2: Setting Up Your Environment

To begin writing scripts using DeepSeek-v3's API, you'll need to set up a development environment. This typically involves:

- **Selecting a Programming Language**: Popular languages for API integration include Python, JavaScript, and Ruby. Python is often preferred due to its robust libraries and ease of use.
- **Installing Dependencies**: If you're using Python, you'll want to install libraries such as requests to handle HTTP requests or pandas for data manipulation.
- **Obtaining API Keys**: Sign up for an API key through DeepSeek-v3's platform to authenticate your requests.

Step 3: Writing Your First Script

Here's an example of a **Python script** that uses DeepSeek-v3's API to automate a search and return the results.

```python
CopierModifier
import requests
import json

# Define the base URL and the endpoint for a
search query
```

```python
base_url = 'https://api.deepseek-v3.com/v1'
search_endpoint = '/search'

# Set up your authentication details
api_key = 'your_api_key_here'

# Define the search parameters (can be
customized based on needs)
params = {
    'query': 'machine learning trends',
    'filters': {'date': '2025'},
    'limit': 10
}

# Send the request to the DeepSeek-v3 API
response =
requests.get(f'{base_url}{search_endpoint}',
headers={'Authorization':    f'Bearer  {api_key}'},
params=params)

# Check if the request was successful
if response.status_code == 200:
    results = response.json()
    print(json.dumps(results, indent=4))
else:
    print(f'Error:            {response.status_code},
{response.text}')
```

This script:

1. Sends a request to the DeepSeek-v3 API with the specified search query.
2. Includes authentication headers using the API key.
3. Outputs the results in a formatted JSON structure.

You can adapt this script to handle different queries, integrate it into a larger automation pipeline, or build it into a web application.

Step 4: Handling Advanced Use Cases

DeepSeek-v3's API can also handle more complex use cases, such as:

- **Batch Processing**: Run multiple searches in parallel or process large datasets.
- **Real-Time Data Retrieval**: Set up webhooks to retrieve results in real time when new data becomes available.
- **Custom Analytics**: Use the results of your searches to generate custom reports or analytics.

Chapter 7: Monitoring and Analytics Tools in DeepSeek-v3

Analytics Dashboard: Understanding the Advanced Analytics Dashboard

DeepSeek-v3 offers an **Analytics Dashboard** that empowers users to track usage, analyze performance, and measure the impact of their search queries and automated processes. This tool provides real-time insights into the health of your system and the effectiveness of your searches, helping you make data-driven decisions for optimal use.

Key Features of the Analytics Dashboard

- **Search Performance**: See how individual queries are performing. Track metrics such as query success rate, average response time, and search relevance. This feature allows you to understand which search strategies are most effective and which areas need improvement.
- **Data Integration Monitoring**: If you're integrating third-party data, the dashboard shows the performance of these integrations, including success rates and any potential issues that might arise.
- **Usage Statistics**: Get a breakdown of your usage patterns, including the number of

searches, tasks, and API calls made within a specific time period. This can help you optimize resource allocation and avoid hitting rate limits.

- **Customizable Metrics**: The dashboard allows you to customize the metrics you want to track, whether it's data quality, the frequency of certain searches, or user engagement.

How to Use the Analytics Dashboard

1. **Navigating the Dashboard**: The main dashboard interface is organized into various sections, including search performance, system health, and integration monitoring. Familiarize yourself with the layout to quickly access the data most important to you.

2. **Interpreting the Data**: Understand key metrics like search latency, error rates, and query success rates. If there are spikes in latency or errors, you can pinpoint specific searches or processes that are causing performance issues.

3. **Setting Alerts**: You can set up alerts to notify you of any significant changes in system performance or usage patterns. For example, if the system detects an unusually high number of errors or queries, you can

receive an email or push notification to address it immediately.

By regularly reviewing the Analytics Dashboard, you can gain insights into how your DeepSeek-v3 setup is performing and make improvements to enhance overall efficiency.

Real-time Monitoring: Using the Real-time Monitoring Feature for Immediate Feedback on Tasks

Real-time monitoring is an invaluable feature in **DeepSeek-v3**, providing immediate feedback on ongoing tasks and search queries. Whether you're running batch processes, automating searches, or integrating data, this feature gives you live updates to monitor task status and performance as it happens.

Key Features of Real-time Monitoring

- **Live Search Updates**: Track the progress of ongoing searches, with updates on the number of results retrieved and the time remaining for completion. This is especially useful for long-running queries or batch processes.
- **Task Monitoring**: Monitor real-time progress of automated workflows, including

batch processing tasks, API integrations, and data retrieval from external sources. You can view a live stream of task statuses, from in-progress to completed.

- **Error Detection**: If an issue arises during a search or task execution, the real-time monitoring system will instantly flag it, allowing you to address errors promptly and minimize downtime.

How to Use Real-time Monitoring

1. **Accessing the Real-time Dashboard**: The real-time monitoring dashboard provides an interactive interface where you can see all current tasks being executed. Use filters to focus on specific tasks or queries.
2. **View Task Status**: Each task or query is listed with key details, such as the status (e.g., in progress, completed, failed), the progress percentage, and elapsed time. If a task is taking longer than expected, you can investigate potential issues immediately.
3. **Instant Alerts for Failures**: Set up failure alerts that notify you instantly if a task fails or if performance drops below a certain threshold. This allows for fast troubleshooting, ensuring tasks are completed without significant delays.

By utilizing real-time monitoring, you gain immediate visibility into the health of your system and can resolve issues swiftly, reducing the risk of prolonged downtime or search inefficiencies.

Combining Analytics and Real-time Monitoring for Maximum Efficiency

The power of DeepSeek-v3's **Analytics Dashboard** and **Real-time Monitoring** becomes even more evident when used together. By combining these tools, you can:

- **Track Long-Term Trends**: Use the Analytics Dashboard to look at historical performance data and identify long-term trends or recurring issues. For instance, if certain searches are consistently slow, you can adjust them over time.
- **Fix Immediate Issues**: While you're analyzing trends on the dashboard, real-time monitoring lets you address issues as they arise, minimizing the impact on your operations.
- **Optimize Search Processes**: Use the insights from both tools to fine-tune search processes, optimize resource allocation, and ensure that your queries and

automation workflows are running smoothly.

The combination of **real-time feedback** and **comprehensive analysis** makes DeepSeek-v3 a powerful tool for maintaining optimal performance and delivering consistent, high-quality results.

Chapter 8: Troubleshooting and Optimization Tips

Performance Issues: Common Problems and How to Resolve Them

Despite the advanced capabilities of **DeepSeek-v3**, users may occasionally encounter performance issues that can affect search accuracy or system efficiency. Below are common problems and effective troubleshooting strategies.

Common Performance Problems

- **Slow Search Performance**: One of the most frequent complaints is that searches take longer than expected to process. This can be caused by:
  - **Overloaded System Resources**: If the system runs multiple heavy tasks simultaneously, it may cause slowdowns.
  - **Complex Queries**: Extremely detailed or complex queries can take longer to execute, especially if they involve a lot of data processing or third-party integrations.
  - **Inefficient Filters**: Using too many search filters or filters that are not optimized for your dataset may slow down the search process.

How to Resolve Performance Issues

1. **Optimize System Resources**: If multiple searches are running simultaneously, consider limiting the number of concurrent searches or scheduling them during off-peak hours.
2. **Simplify Queries**: Avoid excessively complex queries. Try breaking large queries into smaller tasks that are easier for DeepSeek-v3 to handle.
3. **Optimize Filters**: Review your custom search filters. Eliminate redundant filters and make sure they are specific enough to avoid excessive data retrieval.

Other Performance Tips

- **Update DeepSeek-v3 Regularly**: Ensure you are using the latest version of the software, as updates often include performance optimizations and bug fixes.
- **Review Third-party Integrations**: If you're integrating third-party data, check the reliability and performance of those sources. Sometimes external data can slow down the system.

Improving Search Accuracy: Fine-tuning DeepSeek-v3 for Even Better Results

While DeepSeek-v3 is designed to provide accurate search results out-of-the-box, fine-tuning certain settings can help improve the quality of results even further. Here are some tips for optimizing **search accuracy**.

1. Refining Search Parameters

- **Query Refinement**: Be precise with your search queries. For example, avoid using overly broad terms. Instead, opt for more specific keywords that better define the data you're looking for.
- **Advanced Filters**: Leverage custom filters to narrow down the scope of your search. The more specific your filters are, the more accurate the results will be.
- **Weighting Factors**: DeepSeek-v3 allows users to assign different importance levels to certain search parameters. Experiment with adjusting the weights of specific factors (e.g., date, location, relevance) to prioritize the most important criteria for your searches.

2. Utilize Machine Learning Enhancements

DeepSeek-v3 leverages machine learning to improve search accuracy over time. By continuously analyzing past search behavior, it learns patterns and can adjust its algorithm to prioritize more relevant results. Here's how to optimize it:

- **Provide Feedback**: After running a search, review the results and give feedback on the quality of those results. This helps the system "learn" and improve over time.
- **Monitor Learning Progress**: Use the Analytics Dashboard to monitor how well the system is improving in terms of search accuracy. Fine-tune the learning algorithms by adjusting certain parameters based on the feedback.

3. Customizing Data Sources

To further improve search accuracy, integrate data from multiple reliable sources. Custom data integrations help DeepSeek-v3 pull more relevant information, especially when searching for niche or industry-specific data. Ensure the external sources you integrate are trustworthy and well-structured to get the best results.

Chapter 9: Best Practices for Mastering DeepSeek-v3

Expert Tips: Tricks and Insights from Advanced Users on Getting the Most from DeepSeek-v3

To truly master **DeepSeek-v3** and harness its full potential, it's essential to learn from the experts who are already leveraging its advanced features to solve complex challenges. Below are some **expert tips** that can help you get the most out of your DeepSeek-v3 experience.

1. Leverage Custom Filters for Precision Searches

Advanced users often rely heavily on custom filters to narrow down their search results to exactly what they need. Here are some ways to make the most of DeepSeek-v3's filtering capabilities:

- **Use Nested Filters**: When dealing with complex datasets, use nested filters to create more granular search criteria. This helps in drilling down to highly specific information.
- **Combine Multiple Filters**: Don't hesitate to combine filters like date ranges, content types, or keywords to tailor your search results. DeepSeek-v3 allows you to create

multi-layered filters that can dramatically improve search precision.

- **Save Filter Sets**: For repetitive searches, save your custom filter sets as templates. This can save time and ensure consistency in your search results across different sessions.

2. Optimize Query Efficiency

Advanced users often focus on improving the **efficiency** of their queries to handle large-scale searches with speed and precision. Here's how to optimize your queries:

- **Refine Queries with Boolean Operators**: Boolean operators (AND, OR, NOT) allow you to narrow or broaden your search. Mastering these operators will help you perform more efficient searches.
- **Use Keyword Synonyms**: DeepSeek-v3's machine learning algorithms can handle synonyms, but specifying alternative keywords can lead to a more comprehensive search.
- **Batch Search**: Use batch processing to run multiple searches in parallel. This is especially useful when you need to process large datasets quickly.

3. Maximize Data Integrations for Comprehensive Results

Integrating **third-party data sources** can expand your search results and add more context to your queries. Advanced users typically integrate several data sources to increase the accuracy and scope of their results.

- **Reliable Data Providers**: Always choose data sources that are trustworthy and well-organized. Sources with incomplete or unreliable data will compromise the quality of your search results.
- **Data Synchronization**: Ensure your data sources are synchronized and updated regularly to avoid discrepancies or outdated information in your searches.

Case Studies: Real-World Examples of Successful DeepSeek Implementations

Let's take a look at a few **real-world case studies** that highlight how **DeepSeek-v3** has been implemented successfully in various industries.

Case Study 1: E-commerce Optimization for Product Search

Challenge: An e-commerce company faced challenges with its product search feature. Customers often couldn't find the exact products they were looking for, leading to frustration and high bounce rates.

Solution: By integrating DeepSeek-v3's **advanced search algorithms**, the company optimized its product search functionality. They used **custom filters** to categorize products more effectively (e.g., price range, size, color, brand) and applied **machine learning-enhanced search** to predict customer preferences based on browsing behavior.

Outcome: Search accuracy increased by 35%, and customer satisfaction improved significantly, leading to a 20% increase in sales.

Case Study 2: Market Research and Data Mining for Financial Insights

Challenge: A financial services company needed a way to sift through massive datasets to uncover hidden trends and opportunities in the stock market.

Solution: They integrated **DeepSeek-v3** with third-party financial data sources and used **batch processing** for large-scale queries. By applying **custom search filters** and machine learning to identify patterns in historical data, they were able to automate the discovery of profitable stock opportunities.

Outcome: The firm gained insights much faster and more accurately, enabling them to make better investment decisions. Their research cycle time was reduced by 40%, and returns on investments improved by 15%.

Case Study 3: Healthcare Data Management and Compliance Monitoring

Challenge: A healthcare provider needed a way to monitor patient records for compliance with changing regulations and detect any anomalies in medical data.

Solution: The company deployed **DeepSeek-v3**'s **real-time monitoring** feature to keep track of incoming patient data and flag non-compliant records immediately. They also used **advanced filters** to create customized compliance reports based on various medical and legal parameters.

Outcome: The healthcare provider was able to streamline their compliance monitoring process, reducing audit times by 50% and ensuring a higher standard of patient data management.

Chapter 10: The Future of DeepSeek and What's Next

Upcoming Features: A Sneak Peek at Future Updates and Features of DeepSeek

As technology continues to evolve at a rapid pace, **DeepSeek-v3** is no exception. The development team is always working to improve the platform's functionality and incorporate cutting-edge features to meet the ever-growing demands of its users. Here's a preview of some of the exciting features and updates you can expect in **DeepSeek-v4** and beyond:

1. Enhanced AI and Machine Learning Capabilities

DeepSeek-v3 already integrates machine learning (ML) to improve search accuracy, but **DeepSeek-v4** will take this to the next level by:

- **Smarter Search Algorithms**: New ML models will refine search predictions and provide more personalized results based on user behavior and preferences.
- **Context-Aware Search**: Future versions will be able to understand context better, allowing you to perform more nuanced queries that go beyond keyword matching.

2. Integration with Advanced Cloud Platforms

The future of DeepSeek includes **seamless integration** with a wider range of cloud-based tools and data storage platforms. This will allow users to:

- **Access Global Data Sources**: DeepSeek-v4 will facilitate the integration of global data feeds directly into the search platform, expanding the reach and accuracy of results.
- **Enhanced Collaboration**: Improved cloud collaboration features will allow teams to share, annotate, and edit results in real-time, improving collaboration and decision-making.

3. Augmented Reality (AR) Search Visualization

One of the most innovative features being explored is **augmented reality (AR)** for search results visualization. With AR, you'll be able to:

- **Visualize Data in 3D**: Imagine performing a search and viewing your results in an immersive 3D environment where you can interact with data points or even navigate through different results in a virtual space.
- **Real-Time Data Interaction**: AR technology will allow you to interact with

real-time data in a more intuitive and engaging way, making it easier to analyze complex datasets.

4. Natural Language Processing (NLP) Enhancements

DeepSeek-v4 will see improvements in **Natural Language Processing (NLP)** capabilities, enabling you to:

- **Query in Natural Language**: Instead of relying solely on traditional keyword searches, you'll be able to ask questions and get precise answers in a conversational tone.
- **Semantic Search Understanding**: DeepSeek will get better at understanding the meaning behind queries, providing results that are contextually relevant even if they don't exactly match the query words.

Preparing for Changes: How to Stay Ahead of the Curve and Integrate Future Improvements

As DeepSeek evolves, staying ahead of these changes will be crucial to maintaining an edge in your searches and optimizing your workflows. Here are some ways you can prepare for upcoming updates and **DeepSeek-v4**:

1. Stay Informed About New Features

The best way to prepare for new updates is by staying connected with the **DeepSeek development team** through their official channels. These include:

- **Release Notes**: Regularly review release notes for updates on new features and bug fixes.
- **Community Forums**: Engage with the DeepSeek community to discuss upcoming features, share insights, and get feedback from other users.
- **Beta Testing**: Participate in beta programs for early access to new features and the opportunity to influence their development with your feedback.

2. Integrate Future-Ready Tools

To ensure smooth integration of upcoming features:

- **Adopt Modular Systems**: Keep your setup flexible and modular so that you can easily integrate new tools or updates without overhauling your entire system.
- **Test Compatibility**: Before major updates, test the compatibility of your current configurations with the upcoming release.

This will help you avoid disruptions when the new version goes live.

3. Invest in Skill Development

The future of DeepSeek will require new skills to fully leverage its advanced capabilities:

- **Learn Machine Learning**: Familiarize yourself with the basics of machine learning and AI as DeepSeek's integration of these technologies becomes more sophisticated.
- **Explore AR and NLP**: Stay ahead by exploring **augmented reality** and **natural language processing** technologies. Understanding these concepts will give you a better grasp of the upcoming changes.
- **Participate in Training Sessions**: Look out for webinars, tutorials, and training sessions from DeepSeek that will help you get up to speed with new features.

Chapter 11: Scaling DeepSeek-V3 for Large-Scale Applications

Introduction to Scaling DeepSeek-V3

As businesses grow and data volumes increase, the ability to scale **DeepSeek-v3** for large-scale applications becomes essential. Whether you're dealing with thousands or millions of data points, DeepSeek's power to handle high-demand queries and process vast datasets effectively is a critical factor for enterprise success.

a. Understanding Scalability in AI Models

Scalability refers to the system's ability to handle an increasing amount of work or its potential to accommodate growth. For AI models like **DeepSeek-v3**, scalability is crucial to ensure that performance remains consistent as the volume of data, the complexity of queries, or the number of users grows. Here are a few key scalability concepts to consider:

- **Horizontal Scalability**: This involves adding more machines or nodes to distribute the workload. In cloud environments, horizontal scalability allows you to scale DeepSeek dynamically to handle more traffic or data.
- **Vertical Scalability**: Enhancing the performance of existing infrastructure,

such as upgrading servers or processors to handle more intensive tasks, can also scale DeepSeek but is often less flexible than horizontal scaling.

b. Why Scaling DeepSeek-V3 is Important for Large Enterprises

Large enterprises generate massive datasets and require high-performance search tools to process them in real-time. Scaling **DeepSeek-v3** ensures that these companies can:

- **Process Larger Datasets**: Enterprise-level data often exceeds the capacity of small-scale solutions. Scaling allows **DeepSeek** to handle big data without compromising performance.
- **Support More Concurrent Users**: High traffic and concurrent users demand scalable solutions to ensure seamless search operations for all users.
- **Maintain Efficiency and Cost-Effectiveness**: With scalable architecture, enterprises can ensure that resources are allocated effectively, optimizing cost and performance as demands grow.

Cloud-Based Deployment

Deploying **DeepSeek-v3** on cloud platforms is one of the most effective ways to scale the system for large-scale applications. Popular cloud providers such as **AWS**, **Microsoft Azure**, and **Google Cloud** offer flexible and powerful environments to run **DeepSeek-v3** at scale.

a. Setting Up DeepSeek-V3 on Cloud Platforms (AWS, Azure, Google Cloud)

Deploying **DeepSeek-v3** on cloud platforms ensures that you have access to high-performance computing resources, storage, and scalability. Here's a high-level overview of deploying DeepSeek on each of the three major cloud platforms:

- **AWS (Amazon Web Services)**:
  - **EC2 Instances**: Choose EC2 instances with adequate processing power to handle DeepSeek's computational needs.
  - **Elastic Load Balancer (ELB)**: Automatically distribute incoming traffic across multiple EC2 instances for increased reliability and speed.
  - **S3 Storage**: Use Amazon S3 for scalable data storage, ensuring that

DeepSeek can handle large datasets efficiently.

- **Microsoft Azure**:
  - ○ **Azure Virtual Machines**: Set up Azure VMs that match DeepSeek's performance requirements.
  - ○ **Azure Blob Storage**: Use Blob Storage for storing unstructured data, such as logs or raw search results.
  - ○ **Azure Load Balancer**: Ensure high availability and scalability by distributing workloads across multiple VMs.
- **Google Cloud**:
  - ○ **Google Compute Engine (GCE)**: Use GCE instances that provide flexible virtual machines for DeepSeek's processing needs.
  - ○ **Google Cloud Storage**: Store large datasets and make them accessible to DeepSeek in a highly scalable environment.
  - ○ **Google Kubernetes Engine (GKE)**: Deploy DeepSeek in a containerized environment for automatic scaling based on demand.

b. Optimizing Performance for Large-Scale Operations

To get the best performance when scaling **DeepSeek-v3** in the cloud:

- **Auto-Scaling**: Set up auto-scaling policies to automatically increase or decrease the number of virtual machines or instances based on traffic and load.
- **Caching Strategies**: Use cloud-native caching solutions like **Amazon ElastiCache** or **Google Cloud Memorystore** to speed up search queries by storing frequently accessed data in-memory.
- **Data Partitioning**: Break down massive datasets into smaller, more manageable partitions that can be processed independently, improving performance.

Distributed Computing with DeepSeek-V3

For truly large-scale applications, **distributed computing** becomes essential to spread the workload across multiple machines or nodes. This allows **DeepSeek-v3** to handle massive datasets and complex queries more efficiently.

a. Leveraging Multi-Node Setups to Enhance Speed and Efficiency

Distributed computing allows you to break down tasks and distribute them across multiple machines. **DeepSeek-v3** can be deployed in a multi-node setup to:

- **Distribute Load**: Each node in the setup processes a portion of the workload, improving the speed and responsiveness of searches.
- **Fault Tolerance**: In case one node fails, the others can continue to process tasks, ensuring that the system remains operational.
- **Increased Throughput**: With multiple nodes working in parallel, you can significantly increase the throughput of DeepSeek, allowing it to handle large-scale operations.

b. Techniques for Handling Massive Datasets

When working with massive datasets, distributed systems like Hadoop or Spark can be used to enhance DeepSeek's processing capabilities:

- **Data Sharding**: Split large datasets into smaller, manageable pieces (shards) that can be processed independently by different nodes.

- **MapReduce**: Use the MapReduce technique to distribute search tasks, aggregate the results, and return them in a unified format.
- **In-memory Processing**: To speed up search queries, utilize distributed in-memory processing systems like **Apache Spark** to handle data in real-time.

Performance Tuning and Optimization

For large-scale applications, performance tuning is vital to ensure that **DeepSeek-v3** operates efficiently under heavy workloads.

a. Fine-Tuning DeepSeek-V3 for High-Volume Tasks

When dealing with high-volume search tasks, fine-tuning the system's settings can improve its performance:

- **Database Optimization**: Index your database to optimize query performance and ensure quick data retrieval.
- **Parallel Processing**: Enable parallel processing in DeepSeek to allow multiple processes to run simultaneously, reducing the time taken to perform large-scale searches.

- **Memory Allocation**: Adjust memory settings to allocate more resources for high-demand tasks, ensuring smooth operation under load.

b. Best Practices for Maintaining System Stability at Scale

To maintain system stability at scale:

- **Monitoring and Alerts**: Use monitoring tools to track system performance, identify bottlenecks, and set up alerts for issues like memory overloads or slow search queries.
- **Load Balancing**: Continuously distribute the workload across your infrastructure using advanced load balancing techniques to prevent any one system from becoming a bottleneck.
- **Routine Maintenance**: Regularly review your architecture, optimize resources, and perform maintenance to ensure that DeepSeek remains scalable and stable over time.

Chapter 12: Security and Privacy in DeepSeek-V3

Introduction to Security and Privacy

As AI technology advances, **security** and **privacy** have become two of the most critical concerns in the deployment of AI systems. Whether you are using **DeepSeek-v3** to handle sensitive business data or personal information, ensuring the safety of that data and respecting privacy regulations are essential.

a. Understanding the Importance of Secure AI Models

AI models, especially those handling large volumes of data, must be secure from unauthorized access, misuse, and cyber threats. As AI applications grow more complex and capable, they also become more attractive targets for malicious actors. Securing **DeepSeek-v3** ensures that sensitive information is protected from exposure, hacking, or misuse. Here's why secure AI models are crucial:

- **Data Integrity**: Security measures maintain the accuracy and integrity of the data being processed.
- **Trust**: Secure systems help foster trust among users, customers, and stakeholders.

- **Regulatory Compliance**: Many industries are governed by strict regulations on data handling and security, which AI systems must comply with.

b. The Role of Privacy in AI Applications

AI applications like **DeepSeek-v3** often deal with vast amounts of personal and sensitive data. Protecting the **privacy** of users is paramount to maintaining ethical standards and adhering to legal requirements. Privacy plays a critical role in AI applications by:

- **Minimizing Data Collection**: Only collecting the data necessary for specific tasks helps reduce potential risks.
- **Ensuring Data Anonymization**: Anonymizing personal data ensures that individual identities are not exposed.
- **Complying with Privacy Regulations**: Regulations such as **GDPR** and **CCPA** require that AI applications respect user privacy and handle data appropriately.

DeepSeek-V3 Security Features

To safeguard data and maintain secure AI operations, **DeepSeek-v3** comes equipped with a variety of built-in security features designed to protect both the system and its users.

a. Built-in Security Protocols and Encryption Methods

DeepSeek employs a range of security protocols to protect data integrity and prevent unauthorized access:

- **End-to-End Encryption**: All communications between users and **DeepSeek-v3** are encrypted, ensuring that data remains secure while in transit.
- **Data Encryption at Rest**: Sensitive data stored in the system is encrypted, reducing the risk of data breaches in case of a security incident.
- **Secure Authentication**: DeepSeek-v3 implements advanced authentication methods, such as **two-factor authentication (2FA)** and **OAuth**, to verify users before granting access to sensitive data.

By employing strong encryption methods and security protocols, **DeepSeek-v3** ensures that data remains protected throughout its lifecycle— from creation and processing to storage and transfer.

b. Managing Access Control and User Authentication

Managing user access is essential to ensure that only authorized users can interact with sensitive data or perform specific tasks within **DeepSeek-v3**:

- **Role-Based Access Control (RBAC)**: Assigning roles to users helps limit access to only the necessary resources, preventing unauthorized access to sensitive data.
- **User Authentication**: Implementing strong authentication measures (e.g., biometrics, multi-factor authentication) ensures that only authorized users can access the system.
- **Audit Logs**: Maintaining audit logs of user activities within **DeepSeek-v3** helps track access and detect any unusual behavior that could indicate security breaches.

Protecting User Data

Protecting user data is at the heart of **DeepSeek-v3**'s security framework. Sensitive information must be handled with the utmost care to prevent unauthorized access and misuse.

a. Techniques for Safeguarding Sensitive Information

There are several techniques that **DeepSeek-v3** uses to safeguard sensitive information:

- **Data Masking**: Masking sensitive fields (e.g., credit card numbers, social security numbers) helps ensure that data is unusable to unauthorized parties.
- **Access Monitoring**: Continuously monitoring who accesses user data and when helps detect potential security threats early.
- **Data Encryption**: Encrypting sensitive data ensures that even if data is intercepted, it remains unreadable without the proper decryption keys.

b. Data Anonymization and Compliance with Privacy Regulations (GDPR, CCPA)

DeepSeek-v3 implements data anonymization techniques to ensure compliance with privacy regulations like the **General Data Protection Regulation (GDPR)** and the **California Consumer Privacy Act (CCPA)**:

- **Anonymization**: Data is processed in a way that removes personally identifiable information, ensuring that individual privacy is protected.

- **Data Minimization**: **DeepSeek-v3** only collects the data necessary for its operations, in compliance with regulations that limit data collection to what is absolutely needed.
- **Data Subject Rights**: In line with **GDPR**, users are empowered to manage their data, including the ability to request its deletion or access, as well as opt-out of data collection where applicable.

Vulnerabilities and Risk Management

Security vulnerabilities in AI systems can lead to data breaches, system downtime, and loss of user trust. Managing these risks is an ongoing process that involves identifying vulnerabilities, mitigating threats, and responding to security incidents quickly.

a. Identifying and Addressing Potential Security Risks in AI Models

Some common risks that **DeepSeek-v3** may face include:

- **Model Inversion Attacks**: Where adversaries try to reverse-engineer an AI model to access sensitive information. This can be mitigated by using differential privacy techniques.

- **Data Poisoning**: Where malicious actors inject misleading data into training datasets to manipulate the AI model. Preventive measures include rigorous data validation and testing.
- **API Vulnerabilities**: Exposed APIs can be exploited by attackers. **DeepSeek-v3** addresses this by ensuring that APIs are protected with strong access controls and encryption.

b. Strategies for Mitigating Data Breaches and Cyberattacks

To mitigate the risks of data breaches and cyberattacks, **DeepSeek-v3** uses:

- **Regular Security Audits**: Frequent audits and vulnerability assessments help identify and patch security flaws before they are exploited.
- **Penetration Testing**: Simulated attacks help discover and fix potential vulnerabilities in the system before they can be targeted by malicious actors.
- **Incident Response Plan**: In the event of a breach or attack, **DeepSeek-v3** has a clear incident response plan to quickly mitigate damage and restore normal operations.

Best Practices for Secure Use of DeepSeek-V3

To ensure the continued security of **DeepSeek-v3**, best practices must be followed in setting up and maintaining the system.

a. Setting Up Secure Environments for AI Models

When deploying **DeepSeek-v3**, it is important to:

- **Use Secure Networks**: Always deploy **DeepSeek-v3** on secure, private networks to minimize exposure to external threats.
- **Regularly Update Systems**: Keep software and hardware up to date with the latest security patches and updates to avoid vulnerabilities.
- **Apply Least Privilege Access**: Ensure that users have only the minimum level of access necessary to perform their roles.

b. Continuous Monitoring and Auditing for AI Security

Ongoing monitoring and auditing are essential to ensure that **DeepSeek-v3** remains secure over time:

- **Intrusion Detection Systems (IDS)**: Set up IDS to continuously monitor for signs of unauthorized access or potential attacks.
- **User Activity Audits**: Regularly audit user activity logs to identify any unusual or unauthorized actions within the system.
- **Security Dashboards**: Implement real-time security dashboards that provide a comprehensive view of system activity, alerts, and potential threats.

Conclusion: Unlocking the Full Potential of DeepSeek-v3

As we've explored throughout this book, **DeepSeek-v3** represents a powerful and flexible tool for anyone seeking to harness the full potential of AI-powered search, automation, and data management. From its intuitive search relevance tuning to advanced features like automation, custom data integration, and API utilization, **DeepSeek-v3** is equipped to meet the needs of both beginners and advanced users.

Key Takeaways

- **Comprehensive Feature Set**: DeepSeek-v3 offers a wide array of features that allow users to optimize search results, integrate third-party data, automate tasks, and leverage advanced analytics to track performance.
- **Security and Privacy**: As we discussed in the chapter on security, ensuring that your **DeepSeek-v3** environment is secure and compliant with privacy regulations is crucial. With its built-in encryption, access control, and monitoring capabilities, **DeepSeek-v3** is designed to help you safeguard sensitive data.
- **Scalability and Future-Proofing**: DeepSeek-v3 is scalable, allowing you to

deploy it for large-scale operations and future-proof your business. Whether you're working with big data, deploying the model on cloud platforms, or using distributed computing to maximize efficiency, DeepSeek-v3 is ready for the challenges ahead.

- **Best Practices and Optimization**: By following the best practices outlined in this book, you can ensure that you're making the most of DeepSeek-v3's advanced capabilities, from performance tuning to continuous monitoring and troubleshooting.

The Road Ahead

As **DeepSeek-v3** continues to evolve, staying informed about upcoming features, updates, and improvements will be essential to keeping your operations at the cutting edge. With AI-driven tools continuing to grow in relevance and power, mastering **DeepSeek-v3** gives you a competitive edge in leveraging AI for a wide range of applications—whether you're focused on enhancing your search capabilities, automating tasks, or scaling for enterprise-level operations.

Remember, this book is just the beginning. The journey of mastering **DeepSeek-v3** is ongoing, and as you continue to explore its capabilities, you'll unlock even more ways to leverage the platform to meet your specific needs.

Moving Forward

- Stay ahead of the curve by experimenting with new features as they are released.
- Apply the insights and strategies from this book to solve real-world problems and create innovative solutions using **DeepSeek-v3**.
- Share your success stories and best practices with the growing community of **DeepSeek** users and contribute to the collective knowledge of the platform.

The possibilities are limitless when you harness the full power of **DeepSeek-v3**—and as you apply the strategies and techniques shared in this book, you'll be well on your way to becoming a master of AI-driven search and automation.

Thank you for embarking on this journey with us, and we look forward to seeing how you use **DeepSeek-v3** to unlock new opportunities, optimize your workflows, and achieve success.

GLOSSARY:

DeepSeek-v3 features
The key capabilities and tools available in DeepSeek-v3.

DeepSeek-v3 tutorial
Guides and step-by-step instructions on how to use DeepSeek-v3.

DeepSeek-v3 setup
Installation and configuration process for setting up DeepSeek-v3.

DeepSeek-v3 API
The application programming interface of DeepSeek-v3 for custom integrations.

DeepSeek-v3 automation
Automating tasks and processes within DeepSeek-v3 to save time and effort.

DeepSeek-v3 optimization
Fine-tuning DeepSeek-v3's settings to improve search performance and efficiency.

DeepSeek-v3 performance tuning
Adjustments made to enhance the speed and capability of DeepSeek-v3.

DeepSeek-v3 troubleshooting
Solutions to common issues and problems encountered when using DeepSeek-v3.

DeepSeek-v3 search algorithms
The advanced search methods employed by DeepSeek-v3 to refine and improve results.

DeepSeek-v3 security
Measures to ensure the protection of data and access control in DeepSeek-v3.

DeepSeek-v3 privacy
Techniques for ensuring the privacy of user data and compliance with privacy laws.

DeepSeek-v3 batch processing
Processing large-scale queries and tasks efficiently in bulk using DeepSeek-v3.

DeepSeek-v3 cloud deployment
Deploying DeepSeek-v3 on cloud platforms like AWS, Azure, or Google Cloud.

DeepSeek-v3 scalability
The ability of DeepSeek-v3 to handle increasing amounts of data or growing usage needs.

DeepSeek-v3 data integration
Incorporating external data sources into DeepSeek-v3 for enriched search results.

DeepSeek-v3 real-time monitoring
Live tracking of system performance and operations while using DeepSeek-v3.

DeepSeek-v3 distributed computing
Utilizing multiple computers to share the processing load and improve efficiency.

Advanced DeepSeek-v3
Expert-level features and techniques for getting the most out of DeepSeek-v3.

DeepSeek-v3 expert tips
Insights and strategies from experienced users on mastering DeepSeek-v3.

Mastering DeepSeek-v3
Becoming highly proficient in using all features and capabilities of DeepSeek-v3.

DeepSeek-v3 best practices
Proven methods and strategies for effectively using DeepSeek-v3.

Table of Contents